MORE THAN ENOUGH

JESUS IS WHAT YOU NEED!

Pastor Mike Novotny

Published by Straight Talk Books
P.O. Box 301, Milwaukee, WI 53201
800.661.3311 • timeofgrace.org

Copyright © 2018 Time of Grace Ministry

All rights reserved. This publication may not be copied, photocopied, reproduced, translated, or converted to any electronic or machine-readable form in whole or in part, except for brief quotations, without prior written approval from Time of Grace Ministry.

Scripture is taken from THE HOLY BIBLE, NEW INTERNATIONAL VERSION®, NIV®. Copyright © 1973, 1978, 1984, 2011 by Biblica, Inc.® Used by permission. All rights reserved worldwide.

Printed in the United States of America
ISBN: 978-1-949488-06-7

TIME OF GRACE *and* IT ALL STARTS NOW *are registered marks of Time of Grace Ministry.*

Contents

Introduction 5

We Believe in JESUS! 7

JESUS Changes People 16

JESUS Fills You Up 28

Sink Your Roots Into JESUS 40

We Need JESUS, Who Gives Us a Maker's Dozen 51

Conclusion 59

Introduction

What kind of Jesus do you believe in? That seems like an odd question, but there are lots of Jesuses to choose from. Pop culture, Bible movies, and different religions all offer us a different Jesus to believe in. I've seen movies with smiley Jesus, skinny Jesus, bearded Jesus, and baby-faced Jesus. Social media was abuzz when the *Bible* miniseries cast Argentinian actor Juan Pablo Di Pace to play Jesus—some ladies call him dreamy Jesus. *Family Guy* gave us irreverent cartoon Jesus. In the movie *Talladega Nights*, Ricky Bobby loved 8 pound, 6 ounce baby Jesus, and his friend Cal preferred a Jesus in a tuxedo T-shirt. Mormons believe in the man Jesus who turned into a god. Muslims believe in the prophet Jesus whom Allah sent. Hindus believe Jesus is one of a billion gods. There are lots of Jesuses. So, which Jesus do you believe in?

Our answer to that question is not so much a multiple choice choice (A. a good teacher; B. the Son of God) but the reaction of our hearts. Does your Jesus overwhelm you? leave you breathless? drop you to your knees in worship? Does your Jesus captivate your thoughts? Does your Jesus make every sin, every sorrow, every struggle seem small? Does worry stand a chance against your Jesus? Is your cancer, your divorce, your addiction, your everything dwarfed in the shadow of your Jesus? Well, that depends on what kind of Jesus you believe in.

Thankfully, the apostle Paul has something to say about the *real* Jesus.

We Believe in JESUS!

Two thousand years ago Paul wrote a letter to the Colossians because they didn't know which Jesus to believe in. They had heard about the real Jesus, but then some other dudes highlighted Jesus' name and shrunk it down to 8-point font. "Jesus is okay," they preached, "but worshiping angels, spiritual powers, heavenly rulers, unseen authorities is breathtaking." "You can believe in Jesus," they said, "but do you know the real mysteries of deep spirituality?" They weren't against Jesus + Something, but they weren't content with Jesus = Everything. That's why Paul grabbed his laptop, clicked on the caps lock, and wrote one of the biggest, boldest, and most beautiful descriptions of JESUS you'll find anywhere in the Bible. Check out his words:

"The Son [that's Jesus] **is the image of the invisible God, the firstborn over all creation. For in** [Jesus] **all things were created: things in heaven and on earth, visible and invisible, whether thrones or powers or rulers or authorities; all things have been created through him and for him**. **He is before all things, and in him all things hold together"** (Colossians 1:15-17). Wow! Jesus is the firstborn over all creation. He is bigger and better than any created thing. Anything you can taste or touch or see (and everything you can't) bows to Jesus. Because in Jesus all things were created. There is nothing you will ever enjoy in your entire life that Jesus did not create.

Ever looked up at a thousand stars on a country night? Jesus made that. Ever seen a little toddler and seen the cutest, fattest feet in the history of one-year-olds? Jesus made that. Ever eaten cheese curds so fresh they squeaked on your teeth? Jesus made that. Ever driven a car with your knees so you could play air guitar to "Bohemian Rhapsody"? Jesus made that. Ever looked into the big brown eyes of someone you love? Jesus made that. Ever watched the sun come up with a gourmet cup of coffee? Jesus made the beams and the beans. Sunsets, sex, white sand beaches. Sundae cones, Swedish fish, and smooth milk chocolate. Jesus made all of it. Ever seen an angel? No, you haven't. But if you could see 10,000 times 10,000 angels in heaven, guess who they'd be singing to? The One who created them. All things have been created through Jesus.

"And in him all things hold together" (1:17). Without Jesus, things wouldn't hold together. The elements would come flying apart. The ingredients would fly in a thousand directions. The hydrogen and oxygen in an ice-cold glass of H_2O would rip apart and fly out into the universe if Jesus didn't hold them together. Your dog would jump for a Frisbee and fly into space if Jesus took his finger off the button labeled "gravity." Your body's 30 trillion blood cells, 100 billion brain cells, and 206 bones would unravel if for a single second Jesus stopped holding them together. Atmosphere, air, and orbits only work because Jesus tells them to. Science can only be studied because Jesus keeps constants constant. Jesus is the Creator who holds together creation. That's Paul's Jesus. That's the real JESUS. *Jesus is the God of creation.*

If you ever stop by my office, you'll see a block on my bookshelf that reads, "This." A few years ago, my wife and I came up with some family values and "This" was one of our favorites. "This" is our one-word way of remembering that this moment is from God. One weekend we were up

Jesus is the God of creation.

north with some good friends. 83 degrees. Cool water. Romantic sunset. A bag of licorice. And we locked eyes: "This." That weekend we enjoyed coconut shrimp, mojitos, and old-school jams, and I smiled, "This." We parked the boat under a starry sky and just cuddled with the ones we loved, and I felt, "This." And Paul would say, "Yes! Jesus created this. The boat floats because Jesus created buoyancy. Your skin senses the warm sun and the cool water because Jesus made you warm-blooded. Licorice tastes like heaven because Jesus wired your taste buds. Jesus is the firstborn over all creation because all things have been created in him and through him and for him. Everything good in our lives should make us think of this Jesus, the JESUS who is big enough to create all this!

Can I encourage you to connect all of your joy to Jesus? Creation is "for him," so when creation brings you joy, think of Jesus. When the grandkids and the game and the sun and the stars and the food and the friends and the laughter and the love move you, move your thoughts to Paul's words, "Jesus made this." He's that kind of Jesus.

Everything good in our lives should make us think of this Jesus.

But Paul's Jesus gets even bigger. His creation makes him worthy of our worship; look where Paul goes next: **"And** [Jesus] **is the head of the body, the church; he is the beginning and the firstborn from among the dead, so that in everything he might have the supremacy. For God was pleased to have all his fullness dwell in him, and through him to reconcile to himself all things, whether things on earth or things in heaven, by making peace through his blood, shed on the cross"** (Colossians 1:18-20). Boom!

Where do we start with that kind of Jesus?

We could talk about Jesus' incarnation. Paul says, **"God was pleased to have all his fullness dwell in him"** (verse 19). It made God pleased to put all of himself into Jesus. His shocking love. His perfect knowledge. His unstoppable power. Look at Jesus and you see God in sandals, because all of God's fullness dwells in him. Jesus can tell the wind what to do because he's God. He can make people with physical disabilities Hula-Hoop because he's God. He can take a Lunchables and feed a sellout sports crowd because he's God. We call this the two natures of Christ. Fully man, fully God in one person. God with us. That's a big JESUS!

Or we could talk about Jesus' crucifixion. Paul says, **"His blood** [was] **shed on the cross"** (verse 20). We wouldn't expect God to die, but he did. Blood dripped from the crown on his head and leaked from the nails in his hands. The cross was stained with the holy blood of God in the flesh. A God who would die for us? That's a big JESUS!

Or we could talk about Jesus' resurrection. Paul says, **"**[Jesus is] **the firstborn from among the dead, so that in everything he might have the supremacy"** (verse 18). Crucified Jesus showed up outside his own tomb and asked his friends, "Why the long faces?" He appeared behind closed doors and said, "Peace!" He gulped down some fish to prove, "I'm not dead yet." Antismoking campaigns, cutting carbs, and 21-day fixes can help us live longer, but even Richard Simmons is going to die. But not Jesus. He is alive forever and ever and nothing can kill him. That's a big JESUS!

But I don't have time to write about all that stuff. I want to tell you about this: *Jesus is the God of reconciliation.* The reason we love Jesus, praise Jesus, worship Jesus is not because he made sunsets and chocolate. No, the reason Christians worship Jesus is because he is the God of reconciliation.

The reason Christians worship Jesus is because he is the God of reconciliation.

Do you know what that means? Let's imagine things are not good between Mr. and Mrs. Smith. Let's imagine Mr. Smith has been spending too much time mulching flowerbeds and too little time dating his wife. And he's not all that sorry. He's justifying his choices and taking steps away from closeness with his wife. There's distance there, and it's his fault. They need to be reconciled. But what if Mrs. Smith pursues him? What if she buys his favorite perfume? wears his favorite dress? texts him with their favorite inside joke? cooks his favorite meal? reminds him why she is better than a trailer full of mulch and a pocket full of cash? What if she sacrifices her time, her money, her energy to win him back? And what if he turns around? That would be reconciliation!

And that's what Jesus did for you! Paul says, **"Once you were alienated from God and were enemies in your minds because of your evil behavior. But now he has reconciled you by Christ's physical body through death to present you holy in his sight, without blemish and free from accusation"** (Colossians 1:21,22). We were alienated from God. We didn't want to worship him. We didn't want to submit to his commands. In our minds, we wanted what we wanted. But God reconciled us! Jesus took on flesh, was born, lived, died, and rose to win us back. "Who will love you like me?" Jesus pleaded. "Who will forgive you like me? Who will define you like I do? Who will give you a greater purpose? Who will let you live without guilt or shame? Who will give you peace? Who can fix things between you and God besides me?" God calls us, invites us, woos and wins us back. That's reconciliation!

There's more! **"[Jesus] has reconciled you . . . to present you holy in** [God's] **sight, without blemish and free from accusation"** (verse 22). No way! We are presented holy. *Holy* means, "perfect, set apart from sin." When God looks at us, we are set so far apart from our sin that it's not even in his peripheral vision. And without blemish. In 1 Peter 1:19, it says that you were redeemed **"with the precious blood of Christ, a lamb without blemish or defect."** Jesus was without blemish. And without blemish is what we are because of Jesus! Jesus never did anything wrong, never wanted to do anything wrong. Jesus never bit his lip because sin was in his heart. He was perfect. And now we are too. What he is, his people are. Free from accusation. "You're a sinner! You messed up! You disobeyed God! You lied to your parents. You got drunk. You were so jealous. You blew up with your kids. You bad-mouthed your sister." Nope. If Jesus took our sins to the cross, then who will accuse us of being sinners? What can you call me that Jesus didn't take away and nail to his cross? It takes a big ol' JESUS to make a guy like me holy. But that's exactly what I am, and that's what all Christians are. JESUS must be big!

This is the Jesus we worship. Not a small letter *j* jesus. Not the Jesus served with a value meal. No, we believe in the super-sized, galaxy-creating, "this"-producing, conceived of the Holy Spirit, crucified, died, buried, risen from the dead, reconciling the world back to God Jesus. Or, if you want a shorter version: We believe in JESUS! And it doesn't matter what we face—cancer, divorce, back pain, exhaustion, depression, debt, loneliness, addiction, everything—it is always smaller than our JESUS.

That's why Paul urges us to never leave him. You are holy, without blemish, free from accusation **"if you continue in your faith, established and firm, and do not move from the hope held out in the gospel. This is the gospel that you heard and that has been proclaimed to every creature under heaven, and of which I, Paul, have become a servant"** (Colossians 1:23).

Don't move from this kind of Jesus. Don't think there's anything better than the Jesus who gift wrapped every "this" moment and who made sure God has an eternity of these waiting for you in heaven. What could possibly be better than this Jesus?

What could possibly be better than this Jesus?

My prayer is that you never forget this Jesus—the Jesus who stretched out arms of flesh and blood. The Jesus whose love for us proved God's promise, **"I have engraved you on the palms of my hands"** (Isaiah 49:16). Through our Jesus all things were created. Because of Jesus all things hold together. Through our Jesus we are holy, blameless, free from accusation, reconciled to God. That's the JESUS we believe in!

JESUS Changes People

Do people change? Google that question and you'll find yourself in the middle of a heated debate. Sure, everyone agrees some things can change. We're all thankful the mullets and poofy bangs from 1990 prom pictures didn't last! We changed. But I'm not asking you about hair. I'm asking about hearts. I'm asking about hands. I'm talking about beliefs and behavior, about what people think and what people do. Does that, can that, change?

I bet you care about the answer to that question as much as I do. Because you're thinking about *them*. Your sister who isn't sure God even exists. Your husband whose faith is as lukewarm as the dinner you left on the kitchen table. Your classmate whose posts poke fun of your Jesus. Your devoted Muslim friend from Facebook. Your binge-drinking daughter. Your self-centered son. Your teammates who use God's name more than a preacher, but in all the wrong ways. Will they ever change what they believe and how they behave? And will we? If you're not sure about God, will you ever be convinced? If we like drinking beer more than reading a Bible, will we ever get a buzz from God's Word? If we binge and purge or judge guys with colored skin or compare ourselves into death by insecurity, will we ever change? If worry and anger and porn are your three square meals each day, will you ever change? Some folks say a leopard can't change its spots and neither can we. Are they right? Is it possible for people, for them, for us to change? And if so, how?

> **Is it possible for people, for them, for us to change?**

God gives us the answer in the Bible. I want to show you 11 (that's right, 11!) stories of changed lives and the one thing they all have in common. That's three real lives from Bible times and eight from right now that have been changed by the exact same thing.

Here's story #1—Paul. Paul was a terrorist. Ever dared to watch those videos where the monsters in black chop off believers' heads in the name of their god? That was Paul. Paul smiled when his friends bashed in a Christian's head with rocks. Paul posted viral videos, breathing out murderous threats against Jesus' church. Paul hunted down and killed Christian women. But then Jesus showed up, and everything changed. Read this: **"Paul, an apostle of Christ Jesus by the will of God, and Timothy our brother . . ."** (Colossians 1:1). Paul, an apostle of Christ. That Paul? Yup. In fact, that Paul was writing a book of the Bible. It wasn't his first, and it wouldn't be his last. He is the author of half the New Testament. Paul's change was so extreme that the Bible itself admits this: **"When** [Paul] **came to**

Jerusalem, he tried to join the disciples, but they were all afraid of him, not believing that he really was a disciple"** (Acts 9:26). But he *was* a disciple and apostle of Christ. Do you think a card-carrying Al-Qaeda member can change? Ask Paul.

Story #2—The Colossians. Ever seen a PG-13 movie about bad frat boys? That was the Colossians. The Colossians cared more about the keg than about the Christ. They'd stay up all Saturday for Jim (Beam) and Jack (Daniels), but would never wake up on Sunday for Jesus. When Paul wrote to them, he remembered, **"Once you were alienated from God"** (Colossians 1:21). You used to walk in **"sexual immorality, impurity, lust, evil desires and greed"** (Colossians 3:5). But then Jesus showed up. And everything changed. They changed so much Paul could write this: **"To God's holy people in Colossae, the faithful brothers and sisters in Christ: Grace and peace to you from God our Father. We always thank God, the Father of our Lord Jesus Christ, when we pray for you, because we have heard of your faith in Christ Jesus and of the love you have for all God's people"** (Colossians 1:2-4). "Holy, faithful brothers and sisters. We've heard of your faith. Everyone knows the love you have for God's people," Paul said. Wait, those Colossians? Yup. Paul thanked God for their Christian example when he prayed. Do you think frat boys can change? Ask the Colossians.

Story #3—Epaphras. Ever met someone named Muhammad? His parents probably didn't worship Jesus. That was Epaphras. Epaphras was the short version of Epaphroditus. Epaphroditus contains the name Aphrodite. Heard of her? She was the Greek goddess of family and fertility. Epaphras' parents were so religious that they named their son after their favorite goddess. But then Jesus showed up, and everything changed. It seems Epaphras took a trip to Ephesus, where he heard this guy Paul talk about Jesus. And Paul's Jesus was nothing like his parents' goddess. This Jesus was full of forgiveness and love. He didn't demand a sacrifice from us. He sacrificed himself for us. Even though he kept

Jesus was full of forgiveness and love.

his old name, Epaphras left his old faith. That's why Paul told the Colossians, **"You learned** [the gospel] **from Epaphras, our dear fellow servant, who is a faithful minister of Christ on our behalf, and who also told us of your love in the Spirit"** (Colossians 1:7,8). Epaphras became a pastor! A changed Paul changed Epaphras, who changed the frat boys to the faithful. Think your Muslim coworker, your Jewish neighbor, your nature-worshiping cousin can change? Ask Epaphras.

But the stories aren't just from back then. The same thing is happening today all around us.

Story #4—Brian. He's changed. Brian told me,

"After running around gambling and drinking, something/someone knocked some sense into me and brought me back to church. . . . Before I believed God would not forgive me [because of] the pain I caused." But then Jesus showed up. Now Brian enjoys church, attends Bible class, and believes he is forgiven. Think your old college buddy who wasn't the type can change? Ask Brian.

Story #5—Ric. Despite being raised in the church, Ric didn't really get it: "I used to think that if you were a good person, you would get into heaven." But then he went to church. The pastor stood up and said, "We are gonna give you Jesus, followed by more Jesus, and after that there will be more Jesus; and when you think you have had enough, that's right . . . more Jesus." Now Ric says, "I am a blood-bought child of God even though I do nothing to deserve it. I am unconditionally loved, kind, caring, strong, weak, selfish, and giving." Think confused church people can change? Ask Ric.

Story #6—Tara. Tara used to think she would be judged by her past and didn't really know what life is about. But then Jesus showed up. Now she says, "God wants us to spread his Word, and that's a blessing!" Even though she admits it's hard, she believes God is in control, knows what's best, and loves us despite our pasts. Think your friend who isn't all that into Jesus can change? Ask Tara.

Story #7—Brittany. When we discussed her past, she jokingly called herself a "nonreligious redneck," and she lived like it. In high school, a friend told her, "In five years, you're going to be dead." Instead, five years later, she found life. Through a series of events involving the TV program *Duck Dynasty*, a Christian book store, and The CORE (the church where I'm the pastor), she saw something she didn't have, and she wanted it. So she got connected to the Jesus in the Bible and everything changed. Immediately she found it nearly impossible to use God's name like she used to, because that was the God who saved her. "I'm excited to go to church! I love having standards for my relationships! I don't take my own sin lightly," she says now. "What do you think about yourself?" I asked her. "I am a daughter of God. I am beautiful. I am strong in Christ. I am sometimes selfish and unkind, and for that I need Christ," she answered. Think your wandering granddaughter can change? Ask Brittany.

Story #8—Katie. Katie once thought there was no way she could get into heaven: "I thought I was too bad to face God, so I cut him out of my life. But now I know Jesus died for my sins, and he forgives me."

> **"I know Jesus died for my sins, and he forgives me."**

She admits (like every Christian should) that she's still a scrambled mess and confesses, "I'm terrible at forgiveness, but God isn't." Think you're too bad to end up in a better place? Ask Katie.

Story #9—Shane. Shane said, "I once believed the Bible wasn't totally true. I thought people would go to heaven for being good." But something happened last Christmas. He came to church and something changed. Now he says, "I believe the Bible is exactly what it says. I believe life without God is nothing. I am aware of my sins and repent. I believe putting God in the center of a marriage makes a big difference. I enjoy going to church." Think your husband will ever change? Ask Shane.

Story #10—Amna. Amna used to believe humanity was an accident, the Bible was made up, and the church was for crazy people. Now Amna is pining for Jesus! "I am a Bible-loving woman! I love going to church. . . . I love when my son says the Lord's Prayer at church. . . . I believe I am perfectly imperfect. I am whom the Lord made. I am a weak, broken-down sinner, but Jesus came and died for me." Think church is for crazy people? You might change your mind. Ask Amna.

Story #11—Tony. Find some old pictures of Tony, and you'll see gang signs on his hands and money signs on his shirts. The gang was the family Tony didn't have. By age 15, he was witnessing drive-bys, popping pills, and selling cocaine. By age 17, he got a girl he just met pregnant. But

God used the girl, Amna, to save him from the streets. And then last year, God used his Son to save Tony from his sins. Today, Tony is a baptized, Holy-Spirit-filled, every-Sunday-attending man of God. He says, "The gang wouldn't accept me unless I did terrible things. But God accepts me just as I am. Having the Holy Spirit is so much better than all of that." Think the young guys on the streets can change? Ask Tony.

> **"God accepts me just as I am."**

Has God made his case? Can people change? Do people change? Absolutely. They changed back in Paul's day, and they still are changing today. But did you catch how? How do such radical changes happen in beliefs and behavior? Well, did you see what all these stories had in common? In Colossians, Paul says, **"We have heard of your faith in Christ Jesus and of the love you have for all God's people—the faith and love that spring from the hope stored up for you in heaven and about which you have already heard in the true message of the gospel that has come to you. In the same way, the gospel is bearing fruit and growing throughout the whole world—just as it has been doing among you since the day you heard it and truly understood God's grace"** (1:4-6).

Did you catch it? The gospel. The gospel of Jesus Christ. The JESUS I was talking about in the first chapter of this book. The good news of God's grace. The simple fact that God wants sinners. He wants them. His will, his desire, is to love and save and change bad people. God wants terrorists. God wants frat boys. God wants guys named after goddesses. God wants gamblers, gangsters, and nonreligious rednecks. God wants the notoriously bad and the self-righteously good. That's grace. That's what changed Brian and Brittany and Amna. They came to church. They signed up for a Bible class. They got connected to the gospel. And the gospel of Jesus changed them. They simply could not stay the same. Because how can you truly understand love like that and not change?

Do you? Do you truly understand the gospel? If not, let me try one more time. The gospel says God loves you when you don't deserve it. The gospel says when you least expect it, God still loves you. The gospel says when you broke your promise to her, God didn't break his promise to you. The gospel says when you are sitting in a steaming pile of shame, you still smell sweet to God. The gospel says when they don't want you because you don't add enough value to the team, God still wants you on his. The gospel says even though you lived for yourself and were dead in sin, Jesus died for your sins and made you alive to God. The gospel says even though my head is filled with so many unholy thoughts, God still says I am his holy son.

That's the gospel, the message of Jesus who changes people. Faith appears when we hear the gospel. Love is our new desire when we understand the gospel. Jesus' gospel is what changes people.

Here's a new way to think about it. At my house, we have clicker/dimmer switches for our lights. We click on the lights here and use a slider there. Ooh, technology! But this is a perfect example of how things change in the Christian life. And if you don't get this, you will be massively disillusioned with yourself as a Christian and those around you who claim to be Christian. If you're a Christian, at some point God the Holy Spirit flipped the switch of faith. You were enlightened. You heard the gospel, and the light bulb of faith turned on for the first time, "I'm forgiven. I'm good with God. I'm holy because of Jesus." And ever since that day, the Holy Spirit has been working on this dimmer switch called love. I know we all wish our sins and their sins would stop like flipping a switch. Sorry, that's not the Christian life. No, it's a slow change that won't reach full power until heaven. Paul says love is like "bearing fruit," and the last time I checked, fruit doesn't get ripe in a day. It needs day after day after day of the right stuff to grow in small but real ways. That's like our love. Faith happens in a moment. Love grows for a lifetime.

But according to Paul, both changes spring from the gospel.

Please don't forget that or you will forget how much God is changing you. I was at a rap concert once for an artist named Tedashii. I was by far the oldest guy near the stage, and I'm pretty sure Tedashii was looking at me when he joked about the lack of rhythm in the crowd, but I loved the music. What I loved most, however, was his message about change. After a song about the process of growing in love, Tedashii said, "I don't know about you, but I celebrate my sanctification." *Sanctification* is a fancy word for how we change and grow in our Christian love. And we may not be perfect, but we can celebrate it. The slow growth. The little changes. Yes, we still repent of our sins, but with Paul, we thank God for the faith and the love that we see in him and in her and in the mirror, the faith and love that spring from the gospel. We thank God because the gospel is changing people. We thank God that though you used to not come to church, now you do. We thank God you used to live for a buzz, but now you're repenting for it. We thank God you used to worry every day about tomorrow, but now you're learning to trust in God's plan. We thank God you used to ignore the Bible, but now you're trying to

Faith happens in a moment. Love grows for a lifetime.

read it. No, you're not perfect just yet. But you're changing. Because you're hearing the gospel. And the gospel of Jesus Christ changes people.

So I pray you stay close to the gospel. I hope you invite others to hear the gospel. I hope you are bold in sharing the gospel. I pray you go to church on Sunday and try to read God's Word on Tuesday and consider a new Bible class on Thursday. Because you'll hear the gospel. And the gospel changes people.

We thank God because the gospel is changing people.

JESUS Fills You Up

Do you know what one of my best friends is? It's my church directory. It's a booklet that lists a bunch of names, but it's much more than that, because the names remind me of each of my members. Once a week I page through it, and I get emotional. I see Michael, a college-aged kid who still comes to worship almost every week. And I see Jensen, who has a bright future of faith ahead because his mom and his grandma and his uncle and his aunt all care about the Word of God. I see the family whose six kids take up half a page and whose servant's hearts make my church a better place. I see all these names, all these changed lives, and I can't help but thank God for them. The church directory is sometimes my greatest joy of the week.

But it also breaks my heart. Because I see a name, but I never see the face that goes with it and I know that person's faith is shrinking. I see names, and I know some of these people have been fighting and things are tense. I see names, and I know some people are worn out from life's drama. And when I see these names, honestly, I don't know what to pray.

But now I think I do, because I read what Paul prayed for the Colossians. In the previous chapter, we learned that Jesus changed a religious terrorist named Paul into a Christian, and Paul preached Jesus to a goddess-worshiping guy named Epaphras. It changed him, and Epaphras went back to his hometown, Colossae, and preached Jesus to his frat-boy buddies, the Colossians, and it changed them. And eventually Epaphras came back to Paul and told him the news. Paul ran through the directory of this new church, and he thanked God for all the faith and love the gospel produced. But then Epaphras told Paul the bad news. Old habits and new teachings were tempting the Colossians. Their faith and their love were in danger. So Pastor Paul prayed. In fact, he told the Colossians exactly what he was praying for in his letter to them. And this is the same prayer I pray for my members and for you.

Check out what Paul wrote: **"For this reason, since the day we heard about you, we have not stopped praying for you. We continually ask God to fill you with the knowledge of his will through all the wisdom and understanding that the Spirit gives, so that you may live a life worthy of the Lord and please him in every way"** (Colossians 1:9,10). What did Paul want? He wanted the Colossians to live God-pleasing lives. The gospel of Jesus changes people, right? So that means the Holy Spirit works in us to change the way we live as we grow in our faith and Christian love. It's that sanctification concept that I mentioned in the previous chapter. That's what Paul is talking about. So what did the Colossians need? All the wisdom and understanding the Holy Spirit gives. So what did Paul pray? He prayed, "God, fill them! Fill them with knowledge! God, I thank you for who they are, for their level of faith and love, but don't let them stay that way. God, I'm asking you again to fill them up."

"God, fill them! Fill them with knowledge!"

Picture it like a glass half full of water: The Colossians were loving and patient and kind—proof that the Holy Spirit was filling them up with the love of Jesus—but they still sinned in lots of ways—proof that there was plenty of space in their spiritual "cups." Because of the gospel, they knew some amazing truths about God, but they didn't know everything about him. And the Colossians' ability to endure, to hold on to God in their suffering, wavered at times. Because of the gospel, they didn't give up on Jesus, but at times, they thought about it. And the Colossians' joy in their salvation was like that glass. Because of the gospel, at certain times they thanked God for their forgiveness. But at other times, their joy was minimal. So, with this "church directory" in mind, what did Paul pray? "God, fill them up!" In fact, this is what the rest of Paul's prayer is all about (and it's what our prayers should be about too). So let's take some time and unpack each line of Paul's prayer.

First, Paul says, "I'm praying God fills you so you are **'bearing fruit in every good work'**" (1:10). Paul prays for God to fill the Colossians with good works. In his letter to the Galatians, Paul said, **"The fruit of the Spirit is love, joy, peace, forbearance, kindness, goodness, faithfulness, gentleness and self-control"** (5:22,23). So why do you think Paul doesn't just say, "good works"? Why does he call them "fruit"? Because fruit can't grow by itself! Do apples just grow in your grass? Nope, they need a tree. For fruit to grow, it needs to be connected to a source.

And for you to grow, you need to be connected to Jesus—the real Jesus. Jesus said, **"I am the vine; you are the branches. If you remain in me and I in you, you will bear much fruit"** (John 15:5). If we stay connected to Jesus, we will do good works. If we know how he has forgiven us, we will start to forgive others. If we realize how patient he is with works in progress like us, we'll start to be patient with the works in progress around us. When we see how much work Jesus did to make peace with us, we'll start to work to make peace with others. That's the fruit that comes from faith in Jesus. *Because the gospel of Jesus changes us.*

That's what Paul prayed for the Colossians. And that's what I'm praying for you too. Maybe you're a smart young man and you believe in Jesus, so I pray you bear fruit and love your parents.

I pray you show them respect and make these years a joy and not a constant fight. I pray you humble yourself like Jesus and love others. And maybe you're a woman of God who loves going to church. I pray love helps you lose your edge. I pray you become known for kindness, not criticism, for patient Christian love. Or if you had a fight with your family, I pray for your love, the love that is not rude, self-seeking, or easily angered. The love that keeps no record of wrongs. If you're sharp enough to win most debates, I'm praying for your love. Love that listens. Love that doesn't boast. Love that loves not being right but being righteous. I'm praying for God to fill you so you bear fruit in every good work.

But that's not all Paul's praying. Next, he says, "I'm praying God fills you so you are **'growing in the knowledge of God'**" (Colossians 1:10). Paul prays for God to fill the Colossians with knowledge. I thank God you sing, "Jesus loves me this I know," but I pray that's not all you want to know. I want you to know about justification and sanctification and Baptism and Communion and election and atonement. I want you to know more commandments than "You shall not murder." I want you to grow in your knowledge about who God is, what God wants, and what God says about you.

Because knowledge of God changes you. I was at a pizza place in Madison, Wisconsin, with a group of friends, including a professional counselor named Alan. I sat down with three plates filled with pizza, which would have made me a glutton if it wasn't for the tapeworm that lives inside me. Our friend Dan, hoping to jab me, said, "Mike, I didn't know you were buying for everyone!" Smiling, I fired back, "Thankfully I don't need your approval, Dan. I already have God's." (This is how pastors talk trash.) But do you know what Alan, our counselor friend, said? "Mike, if my clients believed what you just said, 90% of them would never have to see me again." That's what growing in the knowledge of God does. Knowing what God says to you and about you isn't just useful for Bible Jeopardy. It's useful for life.

That's why Paul prayed for the Colossians. And that's what I'm praying for you. Jesus organized religion for a reason. I want you to know what love really is and only God can give it. If your heart is in pieces because your boyfriend chose not to be with you, remember the doctrine of election says God chose you! Before he created the world, God chose you. So please do not believe you are unloved, passed by, or worthless. Or maybe you have doubts. I'm praying that you see that God is a good God. He wouldn't lie to you. He only wants what's best for you. I pray you see the connection between his laws and his love. I'm praying for you that you grow in the knowledge of God.

Paul has more to pray. Next, he says, "I'm praying God fills you so you are **'being strengthened with all power according to his glorious might so that you may have great endurance and patience'**" (Colossians 1:11). Paul prays that God fills the Colossians with power. Having the power to endure is not easy. When you feel like the only one in class standing up for what Jesus taught, enduring in the truth is not easy. When your back pain doesn't disappear with a quick prayer, enduring in your trust in God's plan is not easy. When your mother is doing that thing your mother always does, enduring in unconditional love is not easy. No, enduring is never easy.

But did you notice the verb? "Being strengthened." Notice the phrase? "His glorious might." This is not a prayer for a congregational fitness program. This is a prayer for God to strengthen the Colossians. The God who spoke and DNA was invented. The God who once told the Red Sea to become the Red Seas and split in two. The Jesus who treated the wind like a black Lab and told it to sit down and be quiet and it did. Paul is praying, "God, get them through this. They can't do it. But you can. Give them your power, your might, your strength. Because they can do everything through Christ who strengthens them."

That's what Paul prayed for the Colossians. And that's what I'm praying for you. I know your depression is depressing you. You don't think you're going to get through. But I'm praying for God to get at it. I'm praying you believe God's got this. And you. You give so much of your energy to help others. Some days you don't think you can do it another year. But I'm praying for God to fill you up with a renewed passion and the motivation only grace can give. Losing someone you love is the worst. But I'm praying God fills you with great endurance to keep running your race even though your loved one reached the finish line. I'm praying for you that you are strengthened by God so you can endure.

I'm praying for you that you are strengthened by God so you can endure.

And that leads us to Paul's last prayer. He writes, "I'm praying God fills you so you are **'giving joyful thanks to the Father'**" (Colossians 1:12). Paul prays that God fills the Colossians with joy. But how is that possible in a world where we struggle, suffer, sin, and fall short? Let Paul finish! **"Giving joyful thanks to the Father, who has qualified you to share in the inheritance of his holy people in the kingdom of light. For he has rescued us from the dominion of darkness and**

brought us into the kingdom of the Son he loves, in whom we have redemption, the forgiveness of sins" (verses 12-14). Ah! Where do we start? Forgiveness of sins. Redemption. Rescued from darkness. An inheritance in heaven. We could pray for days about such things!

But for now, let's just focus on one phrase—"The Father has qualified you." Being qualified means you're good enough. If you qualify for a bank loan, it's because your credit score and income are good enough. If you qualify for the state track meet, it's because your 800 meter time is good enough. If you're qualified for a job, it's because your education and experience are good enough. In our world, being qualified is all about you. Did you work hard enough? Did you budget wisely enough? Did you study and practice and train enough? Did *you*?

Thank God that God is not like you! Because Paul says, "The Father has qualified you." Not he "might qualify" you if you work hard enough. Not he "will qualify" you if you improve enough. No, the verb is past tense—*has qualified*. Because God took care of making you good enough for his kingdom. That's where Jesus comes in. In Jesus we have the forgiveness of sins. Jesus gave his life for you to forgive your sins, to remove all the reasons God should have disqualified you from his family, his home in heaven. And Jesus gave his life to you, his perfect score, his world record time, his holiness to make you qualified to be a saint and live with the saints in the kingdom of light. That is what moves us and makes us give joyful thanks to the Father!

Ask Tullian. A few years ago, a pastor named Tullian Tchividjian became famous in some Christian circles for his book called *Jesus + Nothing = Everything*, which just so happens to be about . . . Colossians! In it, Tullian tells the story of the agonizing year of his life when he tried to merge his church with an older established church in town. The disaster that ensued robbed him of his joy. A small percentage of the church despised him. They started a petition to remove him as their pastor. Needless to say, he was crushed. *Joy* and *gratitude* were not words that characterized his life. But Paul's words to the Colossians filled him. Tullian says that God showed him that he was attached to human approval. In fact, God set him free with Paul's words in Colossians 1:12: The Father "has qualified you." In other words, God reminded Tullian that there is no need to look for approval from anyone. His value, identity, and worth have nothing to do with what he does and all to do with what Jesus has already done. Tullian's joy and gratitude returned because of Paul's words. And he would need them even more. Tragically, Tullian's marriage and ministry have since fallen apart. He resigned. But his

Twitter profile reveals a man who hasn't forgotten that the Father has qualified him. Tullian tweeted, "So grateful that God is a bottom feeder. . . . I am a persistent promise breaker. God alone is a perpetual promise keeper." Even in the sin and loss, there is joy.

That's what Paul prayed for the Colossians. And that's what I'm praying for you. Maybe you don't think you're good enough. You don't think this gospel is for you. So I'm praying God forces your heart to hear these words: God made you good enough! For the people who lose their joy when they fall back into that sin, as if God's approval of them was based on how long it had been since the last time, I'm praying they see what "has qualified" means. And the person who shared a secret with me from their past. The one that makes then wonder if God could possibly love them. I'm praying God fills them with these words—The Father has qualified you. You will share in the inheritance in the kingdom. I'm praying for you all that you have the constant joy that can only come through the qualifying grace of God.

This is what Paul prayed, "God, fill them with love and knowledge and power and joy! Fill your people." And now I know what to pray for you. And maybe you could pray too. For me. For them.

For us. God, fill us! Fill us with your Word. I thank God you aren't what you were. And I thank God you are what you are. And I'm asking God that what Jesus is you and I will be.

Sink Your Roots Into JESUS

I hate watching Mark's video. Years ago, Mark was one of my favorite stories of God's amazing grace. He was behind bars when we first met, but that couldn't keep the Holy Spirit out. Mark and I talked about the real crime that was our sin and the trial Jesus went through to set us free. And soon after he got out, I baptized him. Our church made a video about his story—a moving video about Jesus' ability to change people. I loved watching that video. Loved. Past tense. Today, that video breaks me. Because Mark isn't walking with Jesus anymore. Only God knows his heart, but all I can see is a man separated from the Word, from repentance, from the community of faith. He embraced a new philosophy on life, but it's not Jesus. The things he once believed, the words he once confessed and we recorded aren't his words anymore.

Do you know someone like Mark? Someone whose faith seemed to fizzle? Someone whose Jesus is a past-tense passion? Do you have a friend, a son, a sister, a someone who used to love Jesus' Word and Jesus worship but gave it up for something else? Or is that someone you? Have you gone through life and found your old faith inferior to your new philosophy? I wouldn't be surprised. Because although we are saved through faith alone, saving faith isn't left alone. It's challenged, questioned, doubted. In other words, Jesus always has competition.

That's why I worry. I know I shouldn't, but honestly I do. I worry about my daughters' faith. I worry about all of you out there with a new faith in Jesus. I worry about new members who are just learning about Jesus. I worry because Jesus has competition. Maybe it's the freshman year world religions course that suggests the Bible is a man-made production. Maybe it's a good friend who prefers to identify as spiritual but not Christian. Maybe it's a YouTube teaching from the Dalai Lama, pushing us toward a less exclusive form of viewing the divine. Maybe it's a TV program where Oprah preaches the only thing not to be tolerated is intolerance.

In our world, there are a thousand teachings that compete with Jesus.

Maybe it's your new yoga instructor who goes back to the spiritual roots of the art. Maybe it's the nicest guy at work who just so happens to be Mormon. Maybe it's a Buddhist cousin or a Karma-loving coworker. In our world, there are a thousand teachings that compete with Jesus.

So how do we protect our faith? How do I protect the faith of my daughters? If you're not a Christian, that seems like an ugly question, I know. It seems defensive, closed-minded, and narrow.

But if I could ask for an open mind, the apostle Paul wants to explain why Christians are so protective of their Jesus.

You see, two thousand years ago Paul heard Jesus had competition in Colossae. The Colossians had come to faith in Jesus, made their new member videos, and gushed about the way Jesus changed them. But then the competition rolled into town, a mash-up of new philosophies and old religions. Some spiritual gurus were pushing a "deeper" form of spirituality. Not the Jesus who came in bodily form and gave his body on a cross, but a more intellectual view of the divine. These gurus loved words like *wisdom*, *mystery*, *understanding*, *knowledge*, *fullness*. Others pushed an experiential kind of faith. Doctrines? The word screams boredom, doesn't it? But what about visions? Visions of angels! Spiritual experiences! Stuff you can feel! That's way sexier than another sermon on another Sunday. Still others pushed Old Testament laws as the way to be saved. Do this! Don't do that! Eat this! Don't drink that! Rules, rules, and more rules. Colossian Christianity had competition. And Paul was worried because ol' Jesus seemed like a flip phone in a touch screen spiritual world. How would Paul protect an endangered Jesus? How would Paul protect Jesus from the competition?

Well, here's what he writes: **"I want you to know**

how hard I am contending for you and for those at Laodicea, and for all who have not met me personally. My goal is that they may be encouraged in heart and united in love, so that they may have the full riches of complete understanding, in order that they may know the mystery of God, namely, Christ, in whom are hidden all the treasures of wisdom and knowledge. I tell you this so that no one may deceive you by fine-sounding arguments. For though I am absent from you in body, I am present with you in spirit and delight to see how disciplined you are and how firm your faith in Christ is" (Colossians 2:1-5). Paul admits there are some fine-sounding arguments out there. There are worldviews that seem more logical, more tolerant, more spiritual, more real. But they can deceive you. Because they're smaller than Jesus. A nickel isn't better than a dime just because it's bigger. And beliefs aren't better than Jesus just because they're newer.

Paul urges, **"So then, just as you received Christ Jesus as Lord, continue to live your lives in him, rooted and built up in him, strengthened in the faith as you were taught, and overflowing with thankfulness"** (verses 6,7). Call him old fashioned, but Paul wants the Colossians to continue with Jesus. Stick with the Jesus you were taught. Build on the Christian foundation you already have. Don't uproot your Jesus. Put down roots in Jesus!

"See to it that no one takes you captive through hollow and deceptive philosophy, which depends on human tradition and the elemental spiritual forces of this world rather than on Christ" (verse 8). "Watch out!" Paul screams with his pen. Your worldview can capture you. Once anything other than Christ determines truth or lie, right or wrong, good or evil, you're in trouble. If your experiences determine truth . . . if any spiritual force besides Jesus becomes your god, you will be taken captive, not with reinforced steel but with your own way of thinking.

Paul gives a few examples of hollow philosophies in Colossae: **"Therefore do not let anyone judge you by what you eat or drink, or with regard to a religious festival, a New Moon celebration or a Sabbath day. These are a shadow of the things that were to come; the reality, however, is found in Christ. Do not let anyone who delights in false humility and the worship of angels disqualify you. Such a person also goes into great detail about what they have seen; they are puffed up with idle notions by their unspiritual mind. They have lost connection with the head, from whom the whole body, supported and held together by its ligaments and sinews, grows as God causes it to grow**.

"Since you died with Christ to the elemental spiritual forces of this world, why, as though you still belonged to the world, do you submit

to its rules: 'Do not handle! Do not taste! Do not touch!'? These rules, which have to do with things that are all destined to perish with use, are based on merely human commands and teachings. Such regulations indeed have an appearance of wisdom, with their self-imposed worship, their false humility and their harsh treatment of the body, but they lack any value in restraining sensual indulgence" (verses 16-23).

Do you see it? The Old Testament isn't better than Jesus. It's about Jesus! Worshiping angels instead of Jesus? The angels worship Jesus! Living for more rules? You died to that, and it doesn't even work! Paul is praying and pleading with the Colossians to keep on with Jesus. Continue in Jesus. Build on Jesus. Sink your roots into Jesus.

> **Continue in Jesus. Build on Jesus. Sink your roots into Jesus.**

What a message for modern Christians! As I was writing this and trying to connect Paul to the present, I got one of those coupon packs in the mail. It had things inside like: "Grand Opening—Psychic Gallery. Psychic Readings—Enjoy the experience of in-depth spiritual readings. Buddhist Meditation—Enjoy the religion and experience spiritual insight. Spiritual Coaching—Gain a deeper insight on life." *Hmm* . . . that sounds familiar.

And then there's Oprah. Millions of people tune

in to watch her. And she doesn't shy away from spirituality. Oprah recorded a series with mystic Eckhart Tolle. Tolle's own website admits, "In Tolle's world, Jesus is not central. . . . Although [he] is not a Christian teacher. . . . Today we need whatever help we can receive to allow the Christian message to take us to a deeper level of transformation" (eckharttollenow.com/article/Spirituality-And-The-Christian-Tradition). And there's this: The Dalai Lama. I'm not sure there is a more lovable-looking man on planet Earth. The Dalai Lama is a symbol of compassion, love, and peace. But what does he teach? The Dalai Lama told *Christianity Today* that Jesus had lived previous lives and his purpose was to help people become better human beings. And then there's this: Karma. The elemental spiritual force of this world. What goes around comes around. What you do determines what the universe does to you. It's a fine-sounding argument, isn't it?

But Paul won't have any of it: Don't let anyone **"deceive you by fine-sounding arguments. . . . See to it that no one takes you captive through hollow and deceptive philosophy. . . . Continue to live your lives in** [Jesus]**"** (Colossians 2:4,8,6). But why? Why is Paul so narrow, so exclusive, so Jesus-only? It's because none of those things can save.

That is Paul's point. The reason Paul calls these philosophies "hollow and deceptive" is not because Oprah is ill-willed or the Dalai Lama is embezzling funds, but because they can't save. "Do this! Stop doing that! Experience this!" can't get anyone out of the hole of sin. But there is One who can. One different from all the rest. One who is more than a hollow shell of laws but has a heart called the gospel.

Paul drops a gospel bomb on the Colossians: **"For in Christ all the fullness of the Deity lives in bodily form, and in Christ you have been brought to fullness. He is the head over every power and authority"** (verses 9,10). You want a spiritual guide? How about Jesus, God in human flesh? You want fullness? How about the fullness of God in a body? How about being brought to fullness, full maturity and holiness in Jesus? You want to worship angels? How about the One the angels worship?

"In [Jesus] **you were also circumcised with a circumcision not performed by human hands. Your whole self ruled by the flesh was put off when you were circumcised by Christ, having been buried with him in baptism, in which you were also raised with him through your faith in the working of God, who raised him from the dead.**

"When you were dead in your sins and in the uncircumcision of your flesh, God made you alive with Christ" (verses 11-13). You want Old Testament rules and laws? How about a new kind of circumcision? Not snipping off a part of your body, but putting off the old you ruled by the flesh? You want a spiritual experience? How about Baptism? The day the old you drowned and a new you was raised with Christ? You want feelings, emotions? How about the feeling of being washed, perfect in the sight of God himself?

"[Jesus] **forgave us all our sins, having canceled the charge of our legal indebtedness, which stood against us and condemned us; he has taken it away, nailing it to the cross. And having disarmed the powers and authorities, he made a public spectacle of them, triumphing over them by the cross**" (verses 13-15). You want laws, laws, and more laws? How about your law-breaking nailed to a cross, paid in full? How about a public spectacle that strips Satan of all his accusations and wraps you in the flawlessness of Christ?

That's Jesus! So how do you protect Christianity? You preach Christ! You give people such a clear view of Jesus that they say, "You want me to leave Jesus for what? For a feeling? For an experience? For a do-it-yourself salvation from Karma Depot? Uh-uh. No thank you. I find my fullness, my faith, my feelings, my spirituality, my religion, my vision, my everything in Christ." If you know Jesus, the *real* Jesus, the big, bold, and beautifully forgiving JESUS, where else would you go? Where else would you want to go?

Paul is pushing us toward a deeply rooted, decades-in-the-making kind of faith. Yes, let's clap for baptisms. But let's not forget the miracle of long-time Christians with deep roots in Christ. It's amazing when lost souls are found. But it's also amazing when found souls are not lost!

This is our goal—JESUS. We don't need more than him. I know it's not earth-shattering for Oprah, but Paul is driving us back to the gospel. So let me give you the most unsurprising homework in church history: Get more of Jesus. How? His Word. If church isn't a regular habit for you, put it on your calendar. If you don't have a way to hear Jesus' Word during the week, sign up for Time of Grace devotions or watch the program online. I know, I know. Not as thrilling as a vision of angels or a concert that "moved" you. But it's the way the Holy Spirit helps you see Jesus. It's the way you put down deep roots so Christ always looks better than the competition.

This is our goal—JESUS.

A preaching professor shared the story of his daughter's wedding. Decades back, the girl planted an apple tree in the family's backyard. As she grew, the tree did too. The trunk stiffened and the branches grew thick and the apples started to grow. But one day a storm hit. The wind rattled the windows and bent the backyard trees over backward. Branches snapped and leaves flew from yard to yard. The little girl was scared, scared for her favorite tree. She pressed her nose against the cold pane of glass and watched, wide-eyed, at her tree. That's where her father found her. He wrapped a loving arm around her waist and said, "Don't be afraid, Baby." "But, Daddy, my tree!" she objected. "Don't worry, Sweetie. It's got roots." He was right. When she walked down the aisle decades later, guess what was tucked inside her bouquet? Trimmings from the apple tree, which had stood and grown over all those years.

And that's my prayer for you. When the wind of new teaching and appealing philosophy blows your way, I pray your roots would be deep in Christ, too convinced of his crazy love to replant yourself in any other soil. Don't be shaken and don't be deceived.

We Need JESUS, Who Gives Us a Maker's Dozen

I don't know about you, but most of the time I'm in desperate need of help. Help with maturing, growing in faith and love and self-control and patience and purity. I don't know about you, but I need a lot of help. Maybe you're new to church and you still have so many doubts. You're not sure God made the world, not sure you're as bad as the Book says, not sure Jesus could forgive what you did. Or maybe you're feeling discouraged. Sober. That was your goal. But then Friday happened. Patience. That was your plan. But then he raised his voice and . . . Trust. You were going to say, "God's got this," but then the shake-up at work. Or maybe it's your status quo spiritual life. You're coming to church. You're praying. But the fire, the passion, the joy isn't there. We need help. We NEED it.

Good news—God wants to help. As I wrap up this book—this study of Colossians—God is going to remind us where to find the help we need for our maturity. In fact, I want to give you God's answer right up front, just in case Facebook has rewired your attention span. Ready for it? We need a Maker's dozen. We need our Maker to give us a group of helpers, a group of supporters, a group that looks out for one another. I need that.

You need that. Paul needed that. The Colossians needed that. Everyone needs that. It's not just nice. God knows we need it.

We need one another. Look at how Paul ends his letter to the Colossians. If you can, count how many people Paul names in these verses: **"Tychicus will tell you all the news about me. He is a dear brother, a faithful minister and fellow servant in the Lord. I am sending him to you for the express purpose that you may know about our circumstances and that he may encourage your hearts. He is coming with Onesimus, our faithful and dear brother, who is one of you. They will tell you everything that is happening here.**

"My fellow prisoner Aristarchus sends you his greetings, as does Mark, the cousin of Barnabas. (You have received instructions about him; if he comes to you, welcome him.) Jesus, who is called Justus, also sends greetings. These are the only Jews among my co-workers for the kingdom of God, and they have proved a comfort to me. Epaphras, who is one of you and a servant of Christ Jesus, sends greetings. He is always wrestling in prayer for you, that you may stand firm in all the will of God, mature and fully assured. I vouch for him that he is working hard for you and for those at Laodicea and Hierapolis. Our dear friend Luke, the doctor, and Demas send greetings. Give my greetings to the brothers and sisters at Laodi-

cea, and to Nympha and the church in her house.

"After this letter has been read to you, see that it is also read in the church of the Laodiceans and that you in turn read the letter from Laodicea.

"Tell Archippus: 'See to it that you complete the ministry you have received in the Lord.'

"I, Paul, write this greeting in my own hand. Remember my chains. Grace be with you" (4:7-18). Tychicus, Onesimus, Barnabas, and Archippus. Demas, Epaphras, Aristarchus, and Jesus called Justus. Nympha, Mark, Luke, Paul. A Maker's dozen. Twelve people God brought together because they needed one another. The Colossians needed Paul's letter of encouragement. Paul needed Tychicus to bring that letter of encouragement. The Colossians needed Epaphras' prayers. Paul needed Jesus' comfort. Archippus needed a kick in the pants. Paul needed his friends to remember his chains. They all needed grace.

Do you know the crazy thing? Paul writes like this all the time. I skimmed his letters and the book of Acts, and do you know what I found? Names. Names. More names. Paul mentions a dozen here. Romans ends with 30 more. And Acts doubles the number. In fact, Paul needed a lot of people. In his books, he listed 91 people by name. To Paul, they weren't just nice. They were needed. He needed them.

I needed him too. Last May I ran the dumbest race of my life. Despite the lazy training, the brutally hot morning, and the 100% humidity, I decided I could run faster than I have in my entire life if I just prayed about it. And it worked. For 16 miles. Unfortunately, I was running a marathon, and the marathon people are kind of picky about the last 10.2 miles. I crashed. I went from flying to walking to almost crying. Within a mile, my pace dropped by a minute (that's bad). By the finish line, my pace dropped by three minutes (that's really bad). Apparently, prayers do not replace preparation! But do you know what happened right in the middle of the crash? Jeremy showed up. Jeremy from my church showed up and started running with me. He was waiting for some friends and decided to help me out. And I got faster. An entire minute faster (that's good). But then Jeremy had to go, and within two miles I was in the fetal position miles from the finish. What happened there? The power of one another.

The Christian life is not a sprint. It's a marathon.

If you haven't figured it out yet, the Christian life is not a sprint. It's a marathon, and your sinful nature is trying to catch you and kill your blessings. That's why we need one another. We need the Jeremys to run with us, spur us on, encourage us when we think we can't. We need that.

But here's the problem. We don't really believe it. We're not sure we "need" one another that badly. They might be nice and all, but we don't need them, do we? While we wouldn't say it, sometimes we live like we're stronger than Paul. He might have needed them. But we don't.

But when we crash, people get hurt. There's more at stake than a few minutes of marathon time. We're talking about his soul. Your coworker. Maybe he's never heard the gospel. Yeah, he went to church as a kid, but all he heard was law. He never heard about the love. And now you've worked with him for four years, and he's still never heard. And unless other people pray, unless the door opens, unless you get the courage, he won't hear. He'll miss the greatest news in the world.

And the kids. They're being scarred. You two are fighting, and they're watching. You're making sure your family tree grows crooked for generations. But you don't air that dirty laundry at church. It's the family secret. But unless they know, unless they pray, unless they correct and rebuke and forgive, it will kill your kids.

And your faith. You've settled. You think 75 minutes on Sunday and relative morality on Monday is all God wants. But you're missing it. You're missing the mission to imitate God and make his name great! Your mind is set on earthly things, and you don't even know it. And unless they know, unless they snap you out of it, unless they spur you on, you'll waste the one life you have to live.

And your guilt. You can't shake it. You feel unworthy, because you know what they don't. You remember the twisted stuff you think. You remember the sin you've been trying to forget.

We need them. We need one another.

But unless they know, unless they can preach the gospel to you, unless they can make you remember God's broom is bigger than your mess, you'll live with that guilt. Oh, please, please don't believe you're okay alone. You're not. I'm not. We need them. We need one another.

This is what God wants for us. This is what we need. We need a Maker's dozen for our maturity. We need people to tell us again and again and again, "Jesus died for that! You know God still loves you, right? Jesus approves of you even now." We need one another to point us to the big, beautiful Savior who was abandoned by his dozen friends so he could die alone and make sure God would never leave you alone. We need them to remind us that our big JESUS will always love, always adore, always accept, and always forgive us. How beautiful to be reminded of the gospel. That's why we need our friends!

Think of it like this: It's not hard to crack an egg.

Give me a pinky finger and a bit of pressure and an egg will crack in a second. Even if it's a jumbo egg, it's still weak on its own. But what happens if I put the same egg with 11 others in a carton? What happens when it's surrounded by a structure? Is it unbreakable? No. But is it stronger? You bet. Can a bit of pinky pressure crack it? No way.

How can you get together with a group like this? Look to your church family. Don't have a church family? Find one! These are friends who gather to talk about this message, our mission, our maturity, to pray and to forgive each other in Jesus' name. It's the best way to connect people to the people they need.

But joining with a group of people isn't enough. You have to be as real as Paul. In a culture that loves to cover up, it's easy to put on the Christian makeup and cover up the stuff we need help with! We ask for prayers for our uncle's cancer instead of our anger. We pray for her move to Michigan instead of our mission. But it doesn't have to be that way. I want you, I dare you, to open up and say, "This is embarrassing, but . . ." And create the kind of groups that change things. The groups where it's okay to not be okay because you already know none of these people are okay. That's what Christians need. That's what I need. You too. We all need a Maker's dozen.

Last week, I needed my Maker's dozen. I got

a letter that I really didn't want to open. It was from a guy who doesn't like my preaching too much. I'm blessed to get tons of encouragement, but this wasn't that. "Just leave the church!" the letter said. But thankfully, it was a Monday—the day I meet with my group. And they were there. My friends. And thankfully my friends have helped me to be real. So they knew how I idolize human approval, how I struggle to handle criticism. But before I opened the envelope, a friend said, "Whatever that says, you know Jesus loves you, right?" And right after I read the letter, she reminded me, "You don't need his approval. You already have Jesus' approval." Those words weren't just nice. They were what I needed. We all do. That's why the Maker gave us one another.

We have a big Jesus who is always by our side. But we also have a Jesus who provides us with the blessing of others to help us on our way as we look forward to heaven.

Conclusion

There are many Jesuses in the world today. Pop culture, world religions, and personal opinions offer us an endless buffet of all types of Jesuses to believe in. At times, the discussion and debate can be exhausting.

Sounds like the culture around Colossae. Spiritual ideas swirled around ancient Asia, threatening the purity of Jesus' identity. Yet, despite the danger, God preserved the faith of his people. Through the passionate preaching of Paul and countless others, the real Jesus survived that century . . . and every century since.

Two thousand years later, people are still wondering about the one called Jesus. Their souls long for something awe-inspiring and glorious, a force powerful enough to forgive, save, and inspire. A miniature Jesus will not satisfy that craving, but the true JESUS will.

So, Christian, live with confidence and lift up the name of the Savior of the world, as confused as that world might be. You believe in the King of kings, the Lord of lords, the Prince of peace, the Son of God, the One whom the whole world is aching for.

You believe in JESUS!

About the Writer

Pastor Mike Novotny has served God's people in full-time ministry since 2007 as a pastor in Madison and now Appleton, Wisconsin. He also serves as a speaker for Time of Grace's video devotions and will be the main speaker of the *Time of Grace* television program after Easter 2019. Mike loves seeing people grasp the depth of God's amazing grace and unstoppable mercy. His wife continues to love him (despite plenty of reasons not to!), and he often prays that Jesus would return before his two daughters are old enough to date.

About Time of Grace

Time of Grace is for people who want more growth and less struggle in their spiritual walk. The timeless truth of God's Word is delivered through television, print, and digital media with millions of content engagements each month. We connect people to God's grace so they know they are loved and forgiven and so they can start living in the freedom they've always wanted.

To discover more, please visit timeofgrace.org, download our free app at timeofgrace.org/app, or call 800.661.3311.

Help share God's message of grace!

Every gift you give helps Time of Grace reach people around the world with the good news of Jesus. Your generosity and prayer support take the gospel of grace to others through our ministry outreach and help them find the restart with Jesus they need.

Give today at timeofgrace.org/give or by calling 800.661.3311.

Thank you!